Numa Hirtz

Purple

Poems

Cover: Created using the Midjourney web app

Publisher: BoD · Books on Demand GmbH, In de Tarpen 42, 22848 Norderstedt

Print: Libri Plureos GmbH, Friedensallee 273, 22763 Hamburg

ISBN: 978-3-7693-0197-7

for the ones whose wings have been clipped

for the ones still folded tightly into their cocoons

for the ones with an ache in their chest

for the ones with insatiable hunger ravaging their insides

for the ones whose ethereal tendrils venture forth into the unknown

for the ones who cannot

Enter, traveler.

I'm me, no doubt,
The mirror of maya
Glitters, full of glee.
Mirth flitters
In the air
as crystals

Pluck them, oh queen
Of mine - How dare I?
Wear them
As shiny tears upon
your cheeks

A peacock, fawn,
spawn of the other,
Attention turned on me
A gaze that burns
I sink

Listen, you,
child no more,
Is this realm gentle? No.

The otherness caresses
And turns my skin cerulean
blue and mossy
A snake curled at my neck
A crowning

Solve et coagula

Insanity
In the driveway
Of my mind

Openings.
Through the ceiling
I see my ghost spread her wings

A day will come, they say.

The pulse of the unseen
Reverberates through me
The fabric of my days
Becomes brittle
Crackles, splinters.
Threads of reason tear
And I taste the sweetness
Of disintegration

Here

Numberless.
How do I remember
what I promised?
Never swim.
Your outlines are lost when
you become one.
Bones
Dust
Who hears?
In the depths of our shared roots
Remembrance
Membranes
Shudder
Stretch
Yawn
Go back to sleep.
Through the veil
A caress

Undo

Through
Eons
Halls
Nobody
Fears
Now
Because they do not know how.
To be blind to the howls of laughter
Bellowing through the
Halls
Eons
Nobody
Fears
Now
Tonight I swim alone.
Down
Down
Down
What will my dive turn up?
Tonight I stare
No shame
Flares of pale flesh
The mirror fields
I nestle into the dark.
I close my eyes.
I become held.

Unlikely hero

My blues taints the air
A breeze of consolation lifts the curtains
And a low rumble rattles the windows

Where is her head tonight?

Iron and salt.
I lick my lips.

Her breath -

I knew then and there.
Nothing would ever be the same.

Hurricanes

How far does my understanding reach?
I wait for the thunderstorm to break.
Unleash your force, oh mighty storm!
Cleanse me, oh rain!
So I may see
Clearly.

Borrowed pain paints me gray.
My hands slowly find their way
Through the rugged landscape of my body.
My hands whisper:
I am.
We are.
She is.
Mother, through me.

Perks and quirks

Jarring
Scarring

Stabbing
Scabbing

Numb and Dumb

Wings beating
In the
Dark
Free feeding
On a
Spark

Lips tightening
Wait for the lightning.

Why so mundane?
Fried my brain.

Giving up, are we?

Tonight
Yesterday, say,
Forever and never –
Tomorrow we braid your hair
If the winds are kind,
and you are born.

I can only walk through one door at a time.
Knock at my door now, will you?

Knee-deep in words

Heads up.
You can do it.
Never falter.
Falter.
This time is as good as any.
Non-existent.

I blurt out:
Self Control is not my forté.

What's with the halted progress?
Why take baby steps when you could be leaping?
Why accept the impairment?

No time is as good as NOW.
Exist, damn it.
Heart
Warm
Snow of my soul

Need knee-deep involvement
Thaw my frozen insides

Never to be molten
Steel
Warm
Steel

Breath
Clouds
On Steel

Melt, damn it.
The trouble lies with the continuum.

Exhale, my love.

Norse

Us.

Myth haunts my days.
My nights are clear as ice,
Nightmares more magical than
The light of day
That threatens to shatter us.

And we sit on the balcony overlooking rooftops
And we eat cake
And the world is beautiful and full of promise
And the streets whisper of secrets, old and new,
and yet to come.

Come, play!
Let's dance!
Across rooftops we dart, safe

Burrow our way
Inside
Into
Into
Into
-

Come, dance!
Let's play!

Suspended
In air
In
In
In
-

Out comes -
Outcome

We emerge.

Alea
Aleathor
Thoric
Torus

Ludus
Luster
Lack
Luster
Blunt
Object
Hope
Hard
Harder
Impervious
Perviously
Impenetrable
Penetrably
Mine

No
Drop it
Let go
Relax the muscles of your palm
Extend your arm
Drop it

No

Under the sea locks slide open
Long-held, held, held
Locks of green sea wisdom hair
Freed, freed, freed at last
Sea wisdom
Taste it
Ingest it
Become it
There! You twirl like locks of sea hair
Liberated
In your element at least, at last

The hum of twilight
Stirs
Three is the charm
No harm, no harm
Who will stir in their sleep?

Upon hearing your hum
Drum drum drum drum

Armoured
Amoured
Enamoured
Armor removed
Simple
A goddess is singing.
A swirl -
Abyss or propeller
Into joy and
Fulfillment?

naught
none
ever
aught
one ever
Interrement, earth enclosing
roots to feed the newborn seed
chest open and heart bared
Barren, bare, betrothed
I surrender the knife to you

Rationality is dragging me to the surface
I gasp and swallow a big gulp of consensus reality.
Gagging, I manage to keep it down.
Salt and bile, a charming aroma.

Rationality combs my wet hair into a slick bun.
And I feel my mind clear.

Focus.

Dreams tickle my feet below the surface.
And I giggle.

How I long to dive and play.

Are your motives pure?
Ulterior? Superior?
Why would I ask?

Was war warranted?
White lies, walls of bodies.
Wilted, whittled to the bone, wary, woeful,
Wounded, wounded, wounded, wounded.

Wounds spiraling through time,
waiting to be witnessed and dissolved.

Fertility

Sometimes there is simply nothing to report.
But the wind carries a promise of rain.

Tomorrow

Never always
Never always
Kinda
Sometimes
Neither nor

Ponder
Wonder
Will I ever

Hysteria and apathy
A sliding scale.

The fragrant soul
Of one unfolding
In innocence

Non sense

Senile
Sensual
Scented
Succulent
Succubus
Blob
Darn

I am afraid of repetition.

A gate

An opening
Into
Here
There
Beyond

Yesterday
Tomorrow
Traveling between layers
Each of us
A potential catalyst

Falling

Unlike
Your hands
Covered
In grief and fur,
kneading the clay
of things
About to take shape

Me
Always seeking depth
But too afraid of falling

What if
I cease to cling
To the edge of the abyss?

A quiet ache

I cannot tell
Nowhere is it written
That you and I are kin

Is kinship what I sought?

A word so old...
Within it echo pain and comfort
Alike.

'What do you seek?', you ask me,
And I hide my blushing face in shame.

Taking it easy

Going slow is permitted.
Being lackluster is permitted.
Being inconsistent is permitted.
Shining bright is permitted.

Return

Join me
At the table
We will eat
Green jelly

Wild nights
And
Restful days

Jest

The day turned sour,
Air turned to thick sad milk,
Perspectives clouded, dour
Futures, a throat coated in silk.

Sing me a song, dear jester!
Distract me, light my day,
So all the wounds that fester
Forget their pain; so far away;

Your song - while healing
might be too much to ask -
It takes me to a kinder world

Where what I do counts as a task of
worth; A cherished feeling;

I need to bathe in nonsensical,
subliminally sensual syllables.

Me, I crave
The sanctity of a sanctuary
The soothing touch of purpose
on my ailing motivation
As I struggle to free myself from the clutches of rot,
The foul smell of stillborn ideas clinging to me,
weighing me down,
slowing me down,
dragging me down.

Sanctity
The word invokes blessings
Oh how sweet

A cesspool of old
versus
A cleansing

A dip in the cool liquid of clarity
For me to come to my senses again.

The touch of mind on mind
Intimate at times

What if
We are all just chemical imbalances
in each other's brains?

Not very poetic.

Lack

Life blows green clouds of generosity at me.
I open my arms,
Hesitantly, expectantly.
The incessant ticking of the clock,
My heartbeat.
I cover my ears, but there is no escape just yet.

The practice of receiving.

The wind.
I decide to
sit with my discomfort.
a little longer. Now. Here. Yes. Breakthrough.

My path leads into the thicket.
Tell me, what do I need to know?
Will I emerge on the other side?
Will I be unharmed or scarred for life?
Will I be changed?

Oh, certainly, the thorns will tear my
clothing until I stumble, naked,
And the spider will weave me a new garment,
fine as cloud.

Why do I ask, if I already know?

Remembrance

I shall buy a small bottle of red to
make blue lotus wine.
My eyes are not without mercy.
One day
Justice comes in long strides
And topples the house.

Sinuous; Our destined paths align,
Lies fall away.
Eyes unburdened, hearts unbound,
An epic sense of destiny breaks through the clouds
and drenches us in hope.

Two

You enter
Unannounced

And yet
And yet
I knew
Roses no wolf has tasted
Crude meat
Cartilage scattered
Crunching under our boots

Conniving splintered factions
Left a smoking trail of burnt earth

My nose knows more than I believe.

A trail. Pick up the scent.
Follow the meandering path, in wavering steps.
Do not fear, my friend.
The dark is merciful.
Its cool fingers caress your aching heart.
The warrior, so spent, may rest their head at last.

Words are a trap.
Their thorns tangle my thoughts.
Wrap it up,
Says the voice.
My gut tells me to keep on.

Beyond reason
Is a place I want to be.

Counterpoint

The day is young
The fire bright
My heart thrums in my ears

The moment filled
To brim with mirth
No doubt, no grief, no tears

The woods, they hum
A song of woe
Dear human child, hear hear

Two melodies
So different
The message though is clear

Eyes of my soul
Behold the truth
Each spore knows life and death

For naught you worry!
Balance
is spun with every breath.

I cross the threshold.
I enter the woods, barefoot. A temple.
The sweet smell of sap and moss greets me.

What is the meaning of the dragonfly?

One hardly ever knows which bird brings death.

Lullaby

Never to be conceived
My darling
Our love is vast and true

But are we being cowards
to try and shelter you?

To keep away the sting of bright lights.
To staunch the flood of choking fear.
To ward off bites of acid truths.

To bar the taint of lies.

To repel souls tormented
by twisted longings and foul hungers.

To guard your peace from waves of dark
foreboding.
To disarm the hands that wield their knives of jest.

To turn from the door the gardener,
who plants the doubt that feeds on your resolve.

To stave off our own spite, wrath and poison.
To keep a leaden cloak of numbness
from becoming your last vestige of sanity.

We'll never, always hold you.

Torn

The iron clasp of obligation
clutches my temples.
The deafening sound of "should"
drowns out all nuance.

Fear fills me.
I fight the flood.
I know I can win.

Her sigh sends a stab of worry through my chest.

Fog

Moments of clarity are few.
For a fleeting instant
I can almost taste the truth.

But to catch it, to hold it,
to feel its outlines and its texture,
to put it in a box, to label it
- a futile endeavour.

I must trust that it will find me
when I need it most.

Null
Void
More alive and cuter than expected.
Are my desires subject to sentencing?

Fleeting glimpses of intoxicating beauty
Stir a desire of the soul,
A longing so deep and sharp
I gasp for breath in surprise.

Daylight and time reveal
the dull gray sheen
I expected to see all along.
But an echo of the deep sharp moment
Hangs in the air. Still.

Null
Void
A breathing seed of myth
cradled by the warm soil of the mundane.

Shifting tides

Over a hill
Under the sea
Rests knowledge
That might unhinge
The world for good.

No other

I am thrown
Back onto myself
My knees buckle
Under the weight

No-one is watching
It really is just me

I catch myself
wishing for a pair of eyes
To rest on me.

Neverending

Upon closure
The act devours itself

Do not hide,
I tell myself.
Do not cower.

You are the one
Who prayed to feel alive
You are the eyes
That begged to see the truth
You are the heart
That trumpeted its hunger
You are the hands
That reached into the light

You enter
Unannounced

And yet
And yet
I knew
Discoveries ahead

My pedestal, at last,
Releases me and turns to dust.
I place my feet, with care
Upon the unfamiliar ground.

Relevance

My teeth turn to dust
While I sleep
The rest of the wicked.

We advance towards another night,
Another round of incubation.

My legs incapacitated,
Mud squelching between my skeletal fingers.

The wind is howling across rows of birch trees,
Young and slender,
Tearing the leaves loose
Into swirling tornadoes of green.

This place
I did not believe existed.
This time
I did not think likely.

But here I am,
Mud caking my face.

Untitled

So maybe I must ask: What can I do for me?

While swimming in the fragile field of reality
becoming,
undone.
Debris
Sharp edges
Morphing
How do I hold on?

So maybe today I ask: What can I do for me?

Nevermind

Today is grainy and slippery all at once
The fluidity of what is real
Makes my head spin uncomfortably

Clacking
Rumbling
Screeching
Discordantly

Can I gather
These disjointed strands
Into a neat braid?

Stranded

Numb and number
Ha ha
A generation on the rocks

Mercury gathering in the pores of conscience
The weight of lead
On our tender shoulders

Purple

No-one should be made to believe my version of events.

Am I to return upon completion of my task?
The deeper I dive, the less I know.
Perhaps I become wider,
able to accommodate more and more layers of the world within me.

To cease expecting praise.
To cease expecting thanks.
To ease into union with the nameless.

See, I wonder:
When my blood turns purple, will I know?
Will I see time snake across the tree's branches?

When I become the world.

Queen

It is dizzying to watch you spin plates
Golden and blue
Your field carries
Your field shields
blow after blow
absorbed; metabolized;
flowers bursting into bloom
atop your temple
your baldachin
offering respite freely
soft emerald moss shelter

an offering
to our naked beaten tired selves

The song of this city.
So discordant, so manyfold
A symphony of stories
A bouquet of attitudes
I move through the wafting clouds of people,
their scents, their noise, their trajectories.
Skin taut, vibrating with alien melodies.
Am I here?

The surprising difficulty of leaving one's own orbit

Fraction
Refraction
Undulation
Regulation
Depth
Found
Concentric path
satellite, traveler
Dominance of the I
Nevermind
I will wait for me
To stop spinning around me

I will come to rest
And turn my gaze outwards

Splinters

Unsavoury, this loss of control,
And yet needed
Piercing
Uncomfortable at best
Unbearably weighty and grey
Affection inflamed

Soothe me

Jackdaw

A new day
A fresh day
So …
Birds on the roof
Their world
A world
I do not know
Comfort in the battering of their black wings
The song of the air
Of rain and wind and moss and tree bark
Of clouds and things I've never seen
A rhythm my body craves.

And if I threw myself against the bars
My whole strength
My whole weight
If I put everything into breaking free

A frantic attempt
Maybe I am blind to the blue sky
The space
The opening behind me
The opening surrounding me

I can
Find the crack in the walls I have built so lovingly
Dissolve the illusion
Be embraced by freedom
Breathe through my skin
Breathe through my roots
Become
Flooded
Until surface tensions are eradicated

A softening

The Shameless Realm I

Define.
Trace me.
Make me flesh.

Broken.
Does the wound close up?
Does the flesh mend?
Break, break into new shapes.

This is due.

Kindred spirits
Huddle together
Despite their formless state.

The Shameless Realm II

An exercise in patience
An exercise in patience
An exercise in detail
An exercise in hunger -

As the wild stallion bucks
Reason looses its grip on his mane
And, sailing through the air,
Surrenders.

A time for patience
A time for patience
A time for detail
A time for hunger -

I cannot break through.
I need to break down first.
Whittle me down
Spread me thin
Knead me
Fine red wax
Porous and breathing,
I let you through.

I let you in.

Fabricate

The wrongness of her touch screams in my bones
But I refuse
To listen

Until the damage is done.

It's easier to read than to write, unless words are pushing up against the top layer of the soil, from beneath, from the underworld, from the unseen and unheard, from the shapeless realm.

The shapeless realm I

Trickle
Tickle

Coo
Woo

Hiss
Kiss
Piss
Diss

Our lives take shape
I wear a cape

Attempts at peace

Like prayer beads

A neat row

Clack
Clack
Clack

The shapeless realm II

My shadow wears a hood.
My shadow wears a gown of dark, soft fabric.
The gown trails my movements.
My shadow is a tall, imposing figure.
My shadow emanates power.

Do I need you to understand?

Being seen is precious,
but not a prerequisite for survival.

The shapeless realm III

I dive into strangeness with fervor.
Push up.
Push upwards.
I push upwards and through
the layer of soil that separates me from the light.
I will not be bound.

Fates collide.
Waves collide.
Shapes change.

Unearth

Celebrate the lure of the incomprehensible
The attraction of a foreign word
So familiar the longing makes your soul wriggle
To break free from the constraints of forgetfulness

New weN

When nehW
Will we ew lliW
Fight? ?thgiF

When nehW
Will we ew lliW
Unite? ?etinU

Now woN

Impose or propose

In dire need
They rock back and forth
As reeds
Notes.
Dire truths.
Hard to open your ears.
Easy to close your heart.
The stark swollen streaks of red
Across the canvas
Lure me into the reeds.
For relief, open.

ADDENDUM

Head under water
Unsee the past
Guilt fills my nostrils
Guilt chuckles behind my eyes
Guilt

Scorch my heart
With mirth and malice
Burn the fields
make them fertile again
I'll empty my heart

Count
Walk and listen
Count
Ever so heavily
On me
On you
On them, even

an empty core

I write a little
and suddenly I can breathe

justification
self-justification
explanation
reason
perspective
When they weigh my heart, will it fly?

Seedling

Nested
Picking up
Where we left off
Signals from the deeper darker denser
Obscured
My rewired
inklings
Obscuring
My beast
twitches
snores

Onwards
We push, we drive
Static answers our
Venture forth brave one on on, on one

Seedlings sinking
Sprinkling inklings
Inking
transitory knowing
Day night
Aim at the crack in between
Who calls?

Time
 Time
  Time
Time time time time
It right

A silver tongue

Tongue in cheek I dance across the map
Unseen melding
Welding us entwined
Vines crawling along
Sprawling
Sliver

red rhyme

Knotted
Not dead
Hung up

Hanging by a thread

Harsh truths
blinding
Enter light

Sandman
Hanged man
Bruise me tight

Upside-down
Our curveball catcher
Topsy-turvy
Bear the blight

Tie a word and buy a will
Softer, deeper
sucker, still

Bust her

Best her
UNLEARN
un learn

Start spitting words, head.

Start churning meaning, heart.

Love given, love taken.
Not a given.

A limp, a lilt, a skip in your step.
Heart of hearts. Hold.
A lisp, a twist, a furtive gesture.
Wait?

When I dare to write the fluttering bird in my palm

When I dare to write ablaze, unafraid of burning

I soar towards the depths

Soot my ink

Guarded no more

Shatter

Where there were no doors before
I can now cross effortlessly
Propelled through, between, ever so gently
My trails becoming bridges

Sol

Nether
Pebbles
I lose the thread
Fate spins it for me
Inner
Sun

A lazy haze
Fog and fumes
Me me me me

When a rhyme finds me
I bow

Stairs

When you are born
ascend
descend
mould
change the shape
of one step
and watch

Doors

fraying; the edges are fraying;
unfulfilled, parched;
exploration is a goal in itself;
data collection;
but thirst tears at our insides.

The stars in the night sky
Early morning sky
Shockingly beautiful
Bright
Incomprehensible
Emanating sounds I am too dull (perhaps too full)
to hear
A veritable symphony, I am sure.

THANK YOU